Bradwell's Pocket Walking Guides

Peak District

BRADWELL
BOOKS

Published by Bradwell Books

9 Orgreave Close Sheffield S13 9NP

Email: books@bradwellbooks.co.uk

British Library Cataloguing in Publication Data: a catalogue record for this book is available from the British Library.

1st Edition

ISBN: 9781910551936

Extracts edited by: Louise Maskill

Design, typesetting and mapping: Mark Titterton

Photograph credits: Mark Titterton

Print: Gomer Press, Llandysul, Ceredigion SA44 4JL To Be confirmed

Maps contain Ordnance Survey data

CONTENTS

FACT FILE

The information in the walk descriptions is produced in good faith, and should be adequate to get you from start to finish, but it is always advisable to take a relevant Ordnance Survey map with you. The correct maps for each walk are recommended in 'The Essentials' sections – the OS Explorer maps are highly detailed maps of a relatively small area (1:25,000 scale, 4cm on the map equals 1km on the ground), while the OS Landranger series are less detailed (1:50,000 scale, 2cm on the map equals 1km on the ground) but show a larger area per map. For these walks the Landranger maps are adequate, and you will need to buy fewer of them to cover all the walks in the book!

All the walks in this book follow rights of way or paths open to the public, with occasional roadside paths (take care when crossing roads). The walks should be suitable for most people, especially families, ranging in length from around 2 to 6 miles. They are also graded and described in 'The Essentials' sections to help you select the most appropriate walk for your party. Walking boots are recommended for all walks, with plenty of insulating layers of clothing and a waterproof jacket and overtrousers if indicated by the weather forecast.

Locations for purchasing food and drink are suggested in 'The Essentials' sections, but are usually located at the start and end points of the walks, so packing a drink and a snack is advisable. Take advantage of public toilets where available!

By law, dogs must be kept on a lead wherever there is livestock, as well as in moorland areas during nesting season and where sheep roam freely. They should also be on a lead if they are likely to be a nuisance to other walkers or cyclists, and certainly when crossing roads. **You should be sure that your dog can manage to get over stiles before you set off on any of these walks; see 'Route' in 'The Essentials' to check whether there are any stiles on the walk you would like to undertake.**

Bradwell Books and the authors have made all reasonable efforts to ensure that the details are correct at the time of publication. Bradwell Books and the authors cannot accept responsibility for any changes that have taken place subsequent to the book being published. It is the responsibility of individuals undertaking any of the walks listed in this book to exercise due care and consideration for their own health and wellbeing and that of others in their party. The walks in this book are not especially strenuous, but individuals taking part should ensure they are fit and well before setting off.

INTRODUCTION

The Peak District was the United Kingdom's first national park, created in 1951. It attracts millions of visitors every year, who enjoy the stunning scenery, picture-postcard towns and villages with historic buildings and ancient customs, a range of outdoor activities such as walking, cycling and climbing, and a wide variety of tourist attractions and museums.

The Peak District National Park broadly divides into two distinct areas, the Dark Peak and the White Peak. The Dark Peak, most of which lies within the northern half of the National Park, is dominated by hills and moors, craggy escarpments called 'edges', rocky tors and deep valleys, some given over to reservoirs. When weathered, the coarse sandstone rock of this area, known as gritstone, grows dark in colour. In contrast, the southern half of the national park, the White Peak, is dominated by undulating upland with a scattering of prominent hills and deep, crag-lined river gorges. The rock here is limestone, which is grey-white in colour.

Documented tourism in the Peak began early, with the publication of Thomas Hobbes' *The Seven Wonders of the Peak* in 1636. Visitors were attracted by the dramatic vistas as well as the reputed healing properties of geothermal springs at the spa towns of Buxton and Matlock Bath. However, the first great increase in visitor numbers came in the Victorian era with the development of rail links that opened up the area to the populations of the great industrial cities of the north. The national park also has a rich industrial history in its own right, with lead- and coal-mining, quarrying and textile manufacture driving the local economy for centuries, but tourism became and remains a vital industry, and there is much for the modern visitor to see and do.

The walks in this book will take you from the gentle slopes and woodlands of the Derbyshire Dales to the wilder, craggier gritstone edges of the northern moors. You will explore picturesque towns and villages, wooded gorges, river valleys and landscaped estates. You will follow ancient packhorse routes, farm tracks and converted railway lines, and you will visit dams, viewpoints and ruined mansions. However, this book only scratches the surface of the walking routes in the Peak District; there are waymarked tracks and long-distance trails aplenty, from the start of the Pennine Way in Edale to the Tissington and High Peak trails, among many others, and the area is criss-crossed with bridleways and public footpaths. Grab this book and some walking boots and start your explorations!

1. TISSINGTON

THE ESSENTIALS

Distance: 2¾ miles (4.5 km)

Route: Easy, no significant ascents or descents, several gates and two stone stiles

Time: Approx. 2 hours

Terrain: Village lanes, the Tissington Trail and a field path

Starting Point: Tissington public car park.
Grid ref SK 177 521, **postcode** for Tissington Hall DE6 1RA

Parking: Pay and display in the public car park

Food and Toilets: The Old Coach House Tearooms in the village; the Bluebell Inn on the Buxton to Ashbourne road just west of the village; kiosk selling refreshments with picnic tables in the car park. Public toilets in the car park

Maps: OS Explorer 1 (Dark Peak) and 24 (White Peak); OS Landranger 19 (Buxton and Matlock)

INTRODUCTION

This very easy walk meanders through one of the most picturesque villages in the country as well as using the Tissington Trail and a footpath through meadows that reveal ancient ploughing patterns.

Tissington is an estate village of stone cottages centred on Tissington Hall, an early seventeenth century Jacobean mansion house. The same family, the Fitzherberts, have lived here since they acquired the original moated manor in 1465, and they continue to manage the estate. The parish church of St Mary, with its Norman tower and font, is the other dominant building in the village.

Tissington is also well known for its annual well dressing. Six wells are decorated during the week of Ascension Sunday (in May or June), with pictures created by pressing flower petals, seeds and other organic materials into a clay base. The pictures usually, though not always, have a Biblical theme. One of the most prominent of the wells is located opposite Tissington Hall.

It is thought the origin of well dressing, now adopted by nearly every village in the Peak District, began at Tissington in 1348 following the village's escape from the Black Death. Villagers attributed this to the purity of water in its wells, and dressed the wells to give thanks for their delivery.

Tissington gives its name to the Trail that passes through the village. Opened in 1971, the Tissington Trail, a walk and cycleway, is now part of the National Cycle Network. It runs for 13 miles from Ashbourne in the south to Parsley Hay in the north, where it is joined the High Peak Trail to connect with Cromford and Buxton. The Tissington Trail follows the course of the former railway line that connected Buxton to Ashbourne, which enjoyed its heyday in the 1930s when it was very popular with ramblers and sightseers. The line offered spectacular views as well as passing close to Dovedale, a popular tourist destination.

1. TISSINGTON WALK

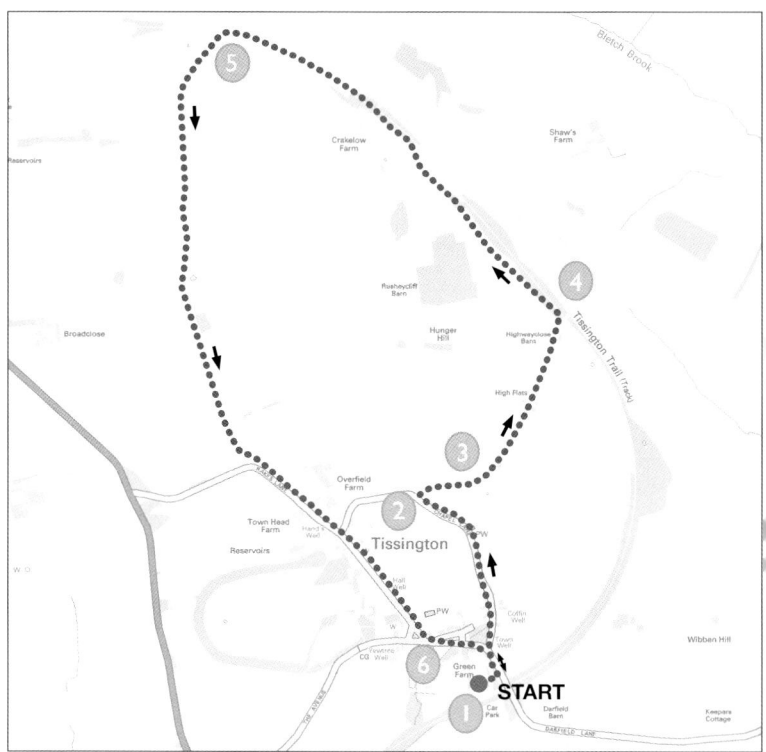

THE ROUTE

1. Leave the car park by the entrance, bear left, then turn right along The Foot. Follow this past cottages and a butcher's shop. Keep straight on after the last buildings – now Chapel Lane – as far as a fingerpost with footpaths going left and right.

2. Turn right, pass through a squeeze stile and gate, cross a small field and exit by a gate onto another lane.

3. Turn right. Continue to where the tarmac ends at a bridge over the Tissington Trail.

4. Do not cross the bridge. Instead, turn right, go through a gate and descend to the Tissington Trail, finishing with a few steps. Turn left, follow the Trail under the bridge, and continue for about ¾ mile to where a footpath crosses the Trail. *There is a particularly good view here of the rolling hills and deep valleys in this part of the White Peak.*

5. Turn left for Tissington and cross the stile on the right of a gate. The path bears slightly right and then becomes a walled track, which may be grassy or muddy depending on the weather. Keep straight on and pass through a gate (or the stile on the left if it is locked). *Notice the 'ridge and furrow' topography in the fields around here. This phenomenon was produced by a system of annual ploughing on the same strip of land used in Europe during the Middle Ages.* Continue across another stone stile by a gate and join The Street. Follow this through the village past the impressive Tissington Hall and the lovely ornate well opposite.

6. Take a left fork in the road after the Old Coach House Tea Rooms, then bear left at the T-junction. Continue past the village pond, turning right into the car park to reach the starting point.

2. HARTINGTON

THE ESSENTIALS

Distance: 4 miles (6.25 km)

Route: Easy, some gradual ascents and one short steep climb out of the dale, some gates, no stiles

Time: Approx. 3 hours

Terrain: Footpaths, a track and a tarmac lane

Starting Point: Market Place, Hartington. **Grid ref** SK 128 605, **postcode** for the centre of the village SK17 0AL

Parking: Pay and display car park in Hartington village (postcode SK17 0BE)

Food and Toilets: Charles Cotton Hotel, the Devonshire Arms and several teashops/cafés. Public toilets opposite the car park entrance

Maps: OS Explorer 24 (White Peak);
OS Landranger 119 (Buxton and Matlock)

INTRODUCTION

This walk follows the River Dove through a winding, wooded gorge, and then takes a high-level route back across the limestone plateau with extensive views of the area.

The starting point for the walk is the village of Hartington, a tourist centre that can get very busy on summer weekends. Close to the River Dove, it is a settlement of attractive stone cottages and several splendid old buildings.

The parish church of St Giles, in its dominating position on the flank of a hillside overlooking the village, dates from the fourteenth century. In the street below the church is the

Old School House, and on the opposite side of the valley is Hartington Hall, a seventeenth century manor house where it is reputed Bonnie Prince Charlie stayed during the Jacobite rising of 1745. Nowadays the manor ranks as one of the grandest establishments owned by the Youth Hostel Association, with a café that is open to the public. Another interesting building is the Old Hartington Cheese Shop, which sells an amazing variety of delicious cheeses.

In the centre of the village one of the hostelries is named after Charles Cotton, who lived at Beresford Hall a mile south of Hartington above the little wooded gorge of Beresford Dale. Cotton was a seventeenth century poet and writer who contributed to his friend Izaak Walton's classic *The Compleat Angler*. The original hall no longer exists as it fell into ruin, but Charles Cotton's Fishing House still survives, almost hidden by trees at the top of the dale. It was erected in 1674 and was designed as a cosy base for his fishing exploits along the River Dove.

2. HARTINGTON WALK

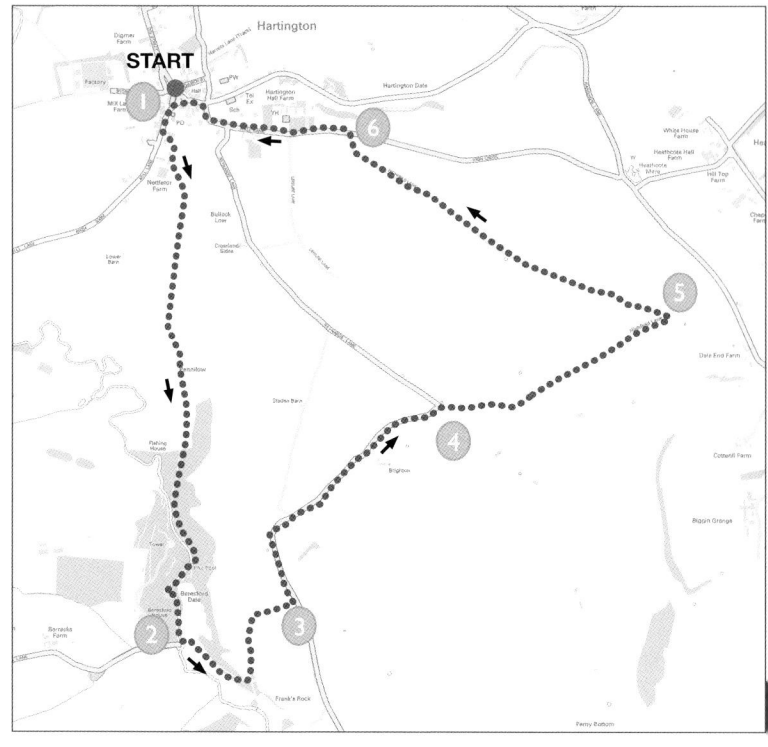

THE ROUTE

1. Walk past the Charles Cotton Hotel in the direction of the car park. Turn left at the public toilets. Pass just left of the building, go through a pedestrian gate and bear right along the footpath. Cross a track via two gates and follow the clear footpath. This descends and passes through an open gateway, climbs a little, and then descends to a gate on the edge of a wood. *Just before reaching this gate, Charles Cotton's Fishing House can be seen across the river.*

2. Continue through the wood and down to join the River Dove as it flows through Beresford Dale. *The riverside path crosses the river at Pike's Pool, named after the pinnacle of limestone that stands on its own in the river like a large version of Excalibur.* Continue downstream from here to another footbridge where a tarmac road meets the river.

3. Cross this footbridge, bear right, and then join the track on the left that runs parallel with the river. Follow this to a metal gate and stile at a crossroads of tracks. Turn left here and follow the walled footpath uphill, steeply at first, to its junction with a lane.

4. Turn left and continue along the lane. This bends right in about half a mile. Continue beyond this bend along the lane to a sharp left-hand bend.

5. Leave the lane at the bend and take the track going uphill signposted to Biggin and Heathcote. This joins another track at a T-junction in half a mile.

6. Turn left and follow this track over the brow of a hill and down to join a minor road. Turn left and follow the road down into Hartington, passing seventeenth century Hartington Hall en route. Turn left at the junction to finish the walk in Hartington village.

3. OVER HADDON

THE ESSENTIALS

Distance: 4 miles (6.25 km)

Route: Easy, some gradual ascents and one steep climb, several gates and two stiles

Time: Approx. 3 hours

Terrain: Riverside footpaths (may be muddy after wet weather) and field paths

Starting Point: Over Haddon car park. **Grid ref** SK 203 664, postcode DE45 1JE

Parking: Pay and display car park, as above

Food and Toilets: Lathkill Hotel and Uncle Geoff's Diner (in season) at Over Haddon. Public toilets in the car park at Over Haddon

Maps: OS Explorer 24 (White Peak);
OS Landranger 119 (Buxton and Matlock)

INTRODUCTION

Starting at an upland White Peak village, the first half of this walk descends to one of the most attractive of the Peak District's limestone dales, following a riverside path past numerous weirs and pools. The return is by a higher level route with great views of the dale.

The walk starts at Over Haddon, a quiet little village to the southwest of Bakewell perched above Lathkill Dale, from which there are extensive views of the surrounding hills and limestone dales. The village has some delightful old stone cottages and an eighteenth century hostelry, the Lathkill Hotel, known as the Miner's Arms until 1896.

Over Haddon has a strong association with lead mining, and the central part of Lathkill Dale, just down from the village, has many relics of this past industry, including the ruins of the engine house of Mandale Mine. In 1854 the "Lathkill Gold Rush" began when 'gold' was struck at a mine in the dale. This soon fizzled out, however, when it was discovered the 'gold' was, in fact, iron pyrites or 'fools' gold'.

At the halfway point along the walk is Alport, an attractive hamlet of seventeenth and eighteenth century stone cottages at an ancient crossing point on the River Bradford. It also has an old water-powered former corn mill that can be seen just downstream of the old packhorse bridge. Although the present building probably dates from the eighteenth century, a corn mill was recorded here as long ago as 1159.

Alport lies on the Portway, which it is thought was one of the most important prehistoric roads in the area, running from Mam Tor in the north of Derbyshire to the outskirts of Nottingham at Stapleford. The village was probably a trading post in Roman times.

3. OVER HADDON WALK

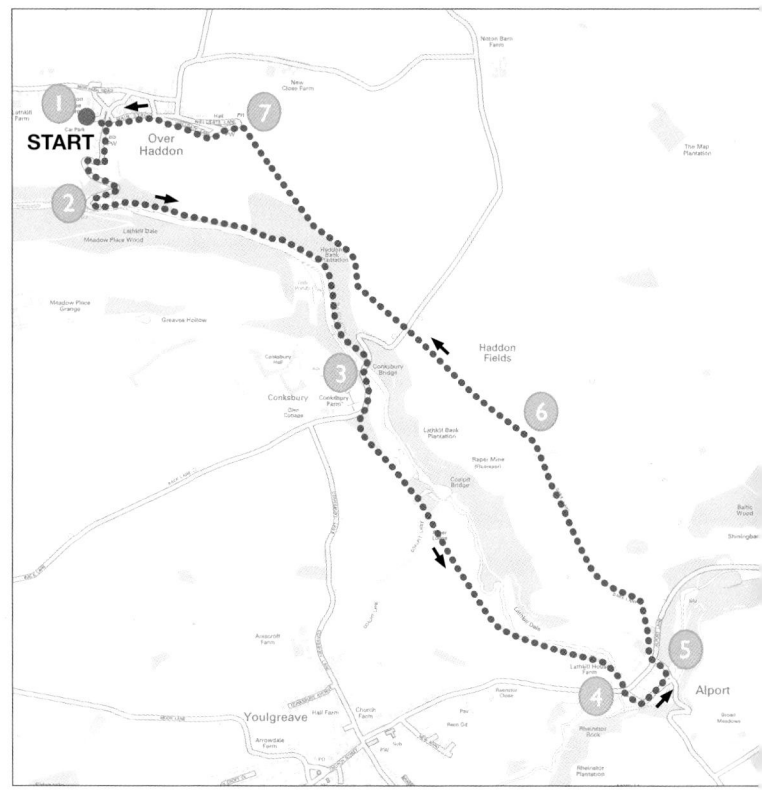

THE ROUTE

1. Exit the car park on the right of the toilets, signposted Lathkill Dale, then descend the steep lane to the River Lathkill.

2. Turn left along the riverside footpath. This climbs at a rocky section, and then passes above the river as it runs through a gorge and drops over numerous weirs. The path emerges at a road on the left of Conksbury Bridge.

3. Turn right, cross the bridge and continue up the narrow lane. On the left of the lane opposite is a footpath with fingerpost. Continue downstream along this footpath, now on the right of the river. Further on the path crosses a track; keep ahead on the footpath to emerge at the road that runs through Alport.

4. Cross the road with care, go left then almost immediately right down the narrow lane between cottages. The lane bends to the left between cottages and delightful riverside gardens, then meets another minor road at a T-junction.

5. Turn left and walk up to the main road. Cross with care and climb the steep tarmac lane opposite. Keep straight on to where it levels out and arrives at a barn. The tarmac ends here and the track can be muddy after wet weather. Continue through the farmyard to a gate on the left with yellow and blue waymarkers and a fingerpost.

6. Pass through the gate, then bear slightly right across the large field signposted to Over Haddon. Cross a stile and the field beyond to arrive at a minor road via a small gate. Cross the road and the squeeze stile opposite, then keep straight on through another gate. Keep ahead, pass through a gate on the right as directed, then bear left up the field. Pass through gates and another field to emerge adjacent to the Lathkill Hotel.

7. Pass in front of the hotel, then bear left at a fork. Follow the lane down past the old village water pump and up to join a higher road, where you bear left to the car park.

4. CHATSWORTH WOODS

THE ESSENTIALS

Distance: 3½ miles (5.6 km)

Route: Easy with a steep climb at the start, some gates but no stiles

Time: Approx. 2½ hours

Terrain: Tarmac lanes and tracks, with the option of some woodland paths where steps are encountered

Starting Point: Chatsworth House car park.
Grid ref: SK 260 703, postcode DE45 1PN

Parking: Chatsworth House car park (small charge)

Food and Toilets: Cavendish Rooms restaurant and other refreshment possibilities at Chatsworth House. Toilets close to the car park

Maps: OS Explorer 24 (White Peak);
OS Landranger 119 (Buxton and Matlock)

INTRODUCTION

A combination of tarmac lanes, tracks and footpaths take you through the exotic and fascinating Stand Woods on the hillside above Chatsworth House. Lakes, a giant rockery and several water features ensure a varied outing.

Chatsworth is the seat of the Duke of Devonshire and home to the Cavendish family since Bess of Hardwick settled here in 1549. Her original house was completed during the 1560s, and was extensively remodelled towards the end of the seventeenth century into the magnificent stately home we see today. The naturalistic setting for the house was the creation of landscape architect Lancelot 'Capability' Brown for the 4th Duke in the eighteenth century.

The more adventurous route to the Hunting Tower takes you past several features that were the creation of the 6th Duke and his head gardener Joseph Paxton in the nineteenth century. These include the aquaduct with its waterfall, and the tumbling stream that begins at another waterfall on the crest of the hillside. The woodland footpaths wind among rocky outcrops of gritstone and an amazing variety of mature and exotic broad-leaved and coniferous trees, which lend a mysterious atmosphere to the woods.

The footpath leads to the Hunting Tower, built around 1582 as a summer house for Bess of Hardwick and now available for rent as holiday accommodation. The view from the front of the tower over Chatsworth is quite magnificent. The three iron cannon are genuine museum pieces and are reputed to have come from one of the ships in Nelson's fleet that fought at the Battle of Trafalgar.

Further along, the walk passes first Emperor Lake, which supplies the water that produces the Emperor Fountain in the grounds of Chatsworth House, and then Swiss Lake, with Swiss Cottage on the far bank.

4. CHATSWORTH WOODS WALK

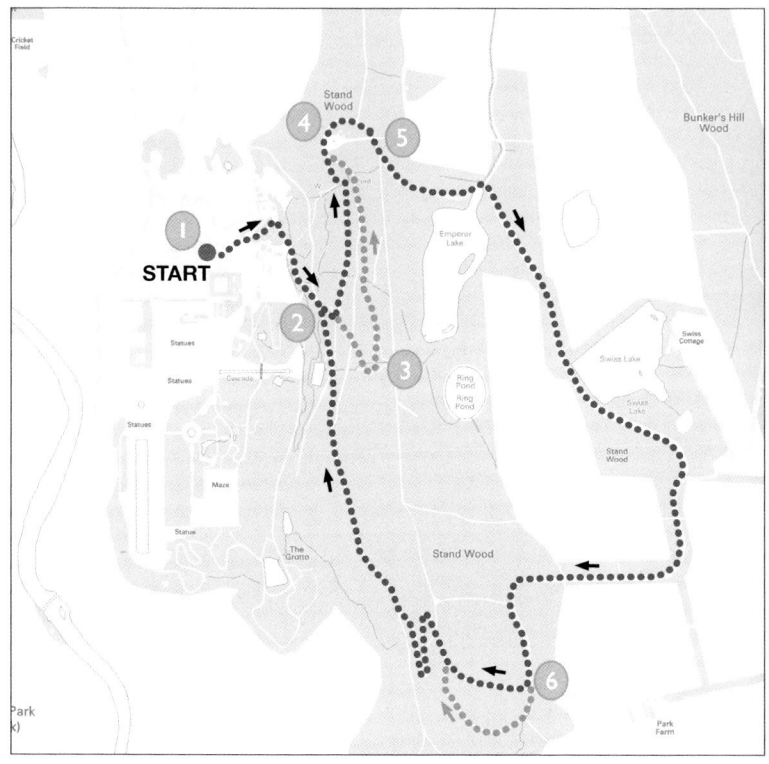

THE ROUTE

1. From the car park walk uphill towards the Farmyard and
    Adventure Playground. On the approach to the Farmyard go
    through the pedestrian gate on the right signposted Stand
    Wood. Continue up the tarmac lane. For the easiest route
    to the Hunting Tower stay on the lane as far as a junction
    with another tarmac lane, turning left to follow this up to the
    Tower.

2. A more adventurous route is to turn left signposted to The Dell, 150 metres or so uphill of the Farmyard. Follow this up to the tarmac lane mentioned above. Cross this and continue straight on up the footpath and wooden steps. Stay on the main footpath as it zigzags steeply uphill on the right of the stream. The last part of the ascent climbs stone steps to the top of a waterfall (close supervision of small children is necessary here).

3. Descend stone steps on the other side of the waterfall, then continue on this level ignoring steps descending to the left, past unusual rock formations and through fairytale woodland, eventually arriving at the sixteenth century Hunting Tower.

4. Facing the front of the Tower, pass it on the right and keep straight on along an earth track, which soon joins a gravel track coming from the left.

5. Turn right here. Follow the main track, ignoring any other possibilities. Pass the top of Emperor Lake and, a little further on, Swiss Lake, easily identifiable by the Swiss Cottage chalet on the far bank. Stay on the main track, forking right at a junction. Eventually a crossroads is reached.

6. **Either** turn right and follow the tarmac lane zigzagging down to Chatsworth House, taking the downhill option at any junctions. **Or** for a more interesting route, go straight across at the junction signposted to Hob Hurst's House and Beeley, but where the track bends sharp left go straight on along a little-used grassy footpath. This bends right shortly and joins the tarmac lane, passing through some ancient woodland on the way. Bear left on joining the lane and continue as above.

Above: View from Monsal Head of the viaduct. **Below:** Chatsworth House

Opposite page: Sheepwash Bridge, Ashford-in-the-Water *(photos: © Mark Titterton)*

5. ASHFORD-IN-THE-WATER

THE ESSENTIALS

Distance: 4 miles (6.25 km)

Route: Easy; apart from the initial climb out of Ashford, any ascent is gradual. Several stiles, but only two are the full height of a wall

Time: Approx. 3½ hours

Terrain: Footpaths and tracks with occasional muddy sections after wet spells. For a short distance beyond Monsal Head the footpath crosses a steep wooded slope

Starting Point: Sheepwash Bridge. **Grid ref** SK 194 696, postcode DE45 1QE

Parking: Ashford public car park off Fennel Street, or considerately on the road between the church and Sheepwash Bridge

Food and Toilets: Aisseford Tearooms, Bull's Head, Ashford Arms; also en route at Monsal Head. Public toilets in the car park

Maps: OS Explorer 24 (White Peak); OS Landranger 119 (Buxton and Matlock)

INTRODUCTION

This walk starts in a picturesque village of stone cottages on the River Wye. A steady but gradual climb along footpaths leads up to the popular viewpoint at Monsal Head. Old walled tracks then lead across open country back down to the river.

Ashford-in-the-Water grew up at a fording point on the River Wye. It was entered in the Domesday Book as "Aisseford", and the tearoom in the village has taken its name from the Old English name for the settlement.

The packhorse bridge known as Sheepwash Bridge has spanned the river near the location of the ford since the early seventeenth century. Until fairly recent times sheep were brought here to be washed before being sheared. The ewes, with halters round their necks, were penned in the walled enclosure adjacent to the bridge. They were then pushed into the river, ducked and made to swim downstream to rejoin their lambs on the riverbank.

Ashford is known for its "Black Marble". Towards the end of the nineteenth century a local industry developed on the edge of the village around the mining of a dark limestone. This turned jet black when polished and was in great demand as an ornamental stone.

The village is also known for the "Maiden's Garlands", made to mark the deaths of virgins until 1801. Some of these are preserved in the parish church which dates from the twelfth century, although much remodelling has taken place over the centuries. Also of interest are the base and stump of a fifteenth century market cross which lie in the churchyard.

En route is the pretty little hamlet of Little Longstone, which has a sixteenth century inn, a seventeenth century manor house and a delightful Victorian chapel. A little further on is the famous viewpoint at Monsal Head with its ice cream vendors, café and hotel.

5. ASHFORD-IN-THE-WATER WALK

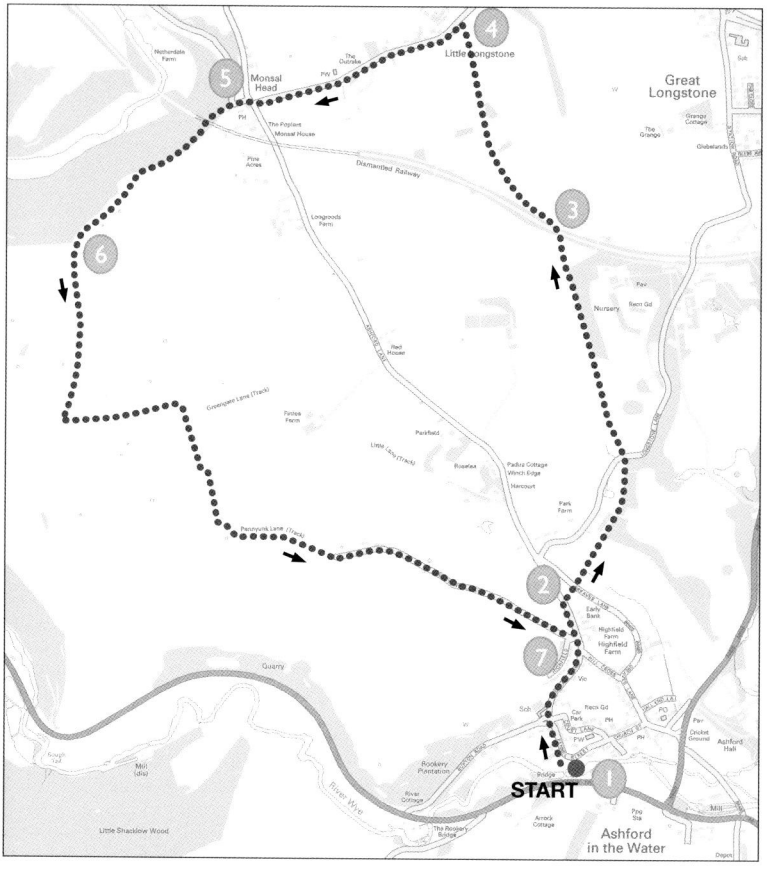

THE ROUTE

1. From Sheepwash Bridge walk up Fennel Street. At the left-hand bend bear right up Vicarage Lane. At the top of the incline keep straight ahead along the lane to a squeeze stile with fingerpost on the right, soon after the sign to Monsal Head.

2. Go through the stile, cross a small field and the stile ahead onto a busier road. Cross with care and take the path almost opposite signposted to Monsal Head. Follow the footpath as it descends, then climbs a little and continues to a minor road. Cross this and the gated stile opposite. Follow the footpath up through several fields with gated stiles, eventually reaching stone steps in a retaining wall for the Monsal Trail.

3. Cross the Trail and take the path signposted to Little Longstone via a stile. Continue up through several fields with gates and arrive at the road that runs through Little Longstone.

4. Turn left and walk along the pavement past the Packhorse Inn. A quarter of a mile further on the pavement ends at Monsal Head. Cross the main road with care and head for the viewpoint at the front of the Monsal Head Hotel.

5. Facing the view, turn left and head for a gap in the wall just beyond Hobb's Café. Pass through the gap and turn left to follow the footpath signposted to Ashford and Monsal Dale. After a short descent, take the left fork signposted to Ashford. This begins as a narrow footpath along a steep, wooded slope, then climbs a few steps before developing into a wider path. Continue to a post with waymark arrows.

6. Bear left at the yellow waymark along the walled and gated footpath. Keep to the waymarked route, which turns sharp left at a gate and descends through a large field before turning right at another gate to resume the former direction. At a footpath junction further on, keep straight on. The footpath eventually becomes a wider track and descends to the top of Vicarage Lane.

7. Turn right, walk down the lane, then bear left down Fennel Street back to Sheepwash Bridge.

6. MONSAL HEAD

THE ESSENTIALS

Distance: 4 miles (6.25 km)

Route: steep climbs on woodland paths. Several gates, one stile

Time: Approx. 3½ hours

Terrain: Footpaths and tracks; short muddy sections are likely after wet weather

Starting Point: Viewpoint in front of Monsal Head Hotel. Grid ref SK 185 716, postcode DE45 1NL

Parking: Pay and display car park at Monsal Head

Food and Toilets: The Stables Bar and Hobb's Café at Monsal Head. Public toilets at the car park

Maps: OS Explorer Map 24 (White Peak); OS Landranger 119 (Buxton and Matlock)

INTRODUCTION

A walk with stunning views and nineteenth century railway architecture, passing through a limestone gorge with a river running through. A combination of footpaths, a high-level track, and the Monsal Trail are used, and there are two stiff climbs up wooded hillsides.

The walk starts at Monsal Head, which draws many tourists for the exceptionally fine view of Monsal Dale, a river gorge with a former railway track running through it. The tortuous route through the gorge, built by the Midland Railway as a scenic attraction, demanded several tunnels and the building of the impressive Headstone Viaduct, also known as the Monsal

Viaduct. The railway line operated from 1863 to 1968, and the track bed is now the very popular Monsal Trail.

The Monsal Head Hotel, formerly the Railway Hotel when the line was in use, would have been a popular stopping-off point for the Victorian visitor, who would have alighted at Upperdale in the valley and been conveyed by horse-drawn carriage up to the hotel.

The River Wye was important during the Industrial Revolution as it powered the cotton mills of Litton and Cressbrook, upstream of Monsal Head. Litton was infamous during the Industrial Revolution for its unscrupulous employment practices, utilising pauper children as indentured labour. Thankfully the scene today is much more peaceful.

After the winding climb through the woods to the farm at Brushfield Hough, there is plenty of opportunity to take in the glorious surroundings. Across the river and dominating the valley is Fin Cop, a hill with steep flanks and earthworks created during the late Bronze Age. Longstone Local History Group have carried out extensive research of the hillfort; excavations during 2009 and 2010 produced finds from a mass grave that included the skulls of females and infants. Barrows and round house platforms were also found, suggesting this was a major settlement during the Bronze and Iron Ages.

6. MONSAL HEAD WALK

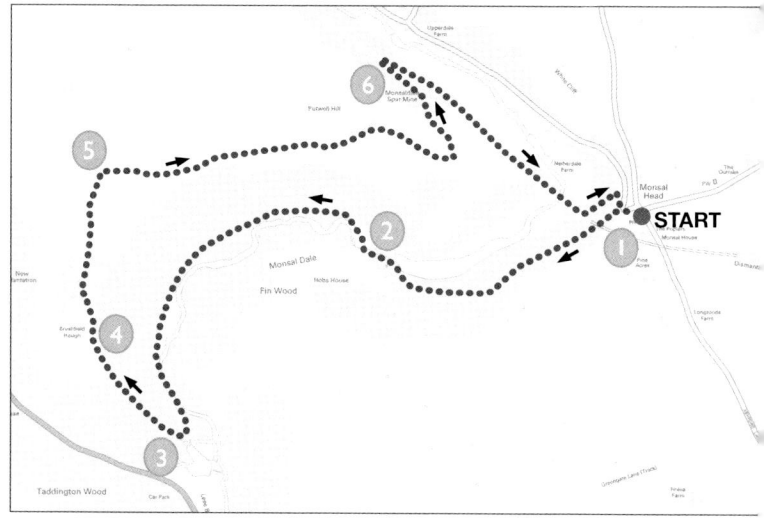

THE ROUTE

1. The walk is described from the viewpoint overlooking the spectacular gorge of Monsal Dale. Facing the dale, go left to the fingerpost just beyond the café and turn left to follow the narrow path signposted Ashford and Monsal Dale. In a short distance the path forks. Take the right fork and follow the descending footpath through woodland, meeting the River Wye at a large and beautiful weir. Cross the river by the footbridge.

2. Turn left and take the path following the river downstream. Either stay on this or take short diversions to follow the riverside – the main footpath gets muddy after prolonged wet weather. Continue down the dale for about a kilometre to a fingerpost on the right.

3. Turn right for Brushfield Hough and follow the steep zigzag path up through woods. Eventually the ground levels off and the path arrives at a stile in a stone wall.

4. Cross the stile and bear right along the track towards farm buildings. On approaching the buildings bear left off the track to a gate. Pass through this and bear left between farm buildings, go through another gateway, then turn right to follow the farm track. Continue through a gate. After the second gateway bear slightly right along a field path and continue to a track.

5. Turn right, go through a gate and follow the high-level track, taking short diversions on the right of the track in wet conditions. Eventually, the track begins to descend after passing a relic of the lead-mining industry. The descent is best taken on the right of the track, which is stony and awkward. Follow the track around a left-hand bend, ignoring the footpath that bears right and descends more steeply to the Monsal Viaduct.

6. Leave the track before it passes under a bridge, bearing right to join the Monsal Trail at the former station at Upperdale. Turn right and follow the Trail to and across the Monsal Viaduct, then turn left just before the tunnel and take the steep path up to Monsal Head for well-deserved refreshments!

Note: for more walks in and around Monsal, see Bradwell's Walking Guide – 8 Walks on the Monsal Trail.

7. BRETTON

THE ESSENTIALS

Distance: 3½ miles (5.6 km)

Route: Medium, with a fairly steep descent to the valley bottom and one short, steep climb out of the valley. Several gates, five stiles

Time: Approx. 3 hours

Terrain: A mixture of tracks and footpaths in undulating terrain, with a short muddy section

Starting Point: Bretton, located on a high country road accessible from Grindleford, Eyam or Foolow.
Grid ref SK 201 779, postcode S32 5QD

Parking: Considerate roadside parking uphill of the Barrel Inn

Food and Toilets: The Barrel Inn at Bretton. The nearest public toilets are in Eyam

Maps: OS Explorer 24 (White Peak);
OS Landranger 119 (Buxton and Matlock)

INTRODUCTION

The walk starts at a hamlet with breath-taking views of the central Peak District, and then uses an ancient trail to descend into a secluded wooded valley. After wending through it, a short zigzag climb up a steep wooded slope takes you back to the higher ground.

In the heyday of lead-mining in the eighteenth and nineteenth centuries Bretton was a more substantial settlement, with a row of miners' cottages between the inn and the present location of the Youth Hostel. The Barrel Inn lays claim to being the highest public house in Derbyshire. Undoubtedly it has the finest views of any Peak District hostelry. The building dates from 1597 but probably did not become a fully-fledged inn until the seventeenth century. To emphasize its historic roots a list of landlords since 1753 hangs on a wall by the bar.

The inn stands alongside what was once the turnpike road from Buxton to Grindleford. The walk starts along Back Lane, an earlier turnpike road replaced by the Buxton to Grindleford route, from which there is panoramic view of the hills and moors of the Dark Peak, with Mam Tor clearly discernible.

Further on, the walk takes you to a former packhorse trail that linked Eyam with Bradwell, dropping to cross the brook in Bretton Clough at a fording point known as Stoke Ford. Along the descent there are stunning views up and down the length of Bretton Clough. The word "clough" means valley with a stream, and there are a number of these in this part of the Dark Peak.

Bretton Clough is very secluded, and in 1745 the farmers of Eyam drove their cattle into the valley to hide them from Bonnie Prince Charlie and his Highlanders on their way south. At this time there were several homesteads in the valley. The ruins of some of these are passed as one crosses the little walled fields.

7. BRETTON WALK

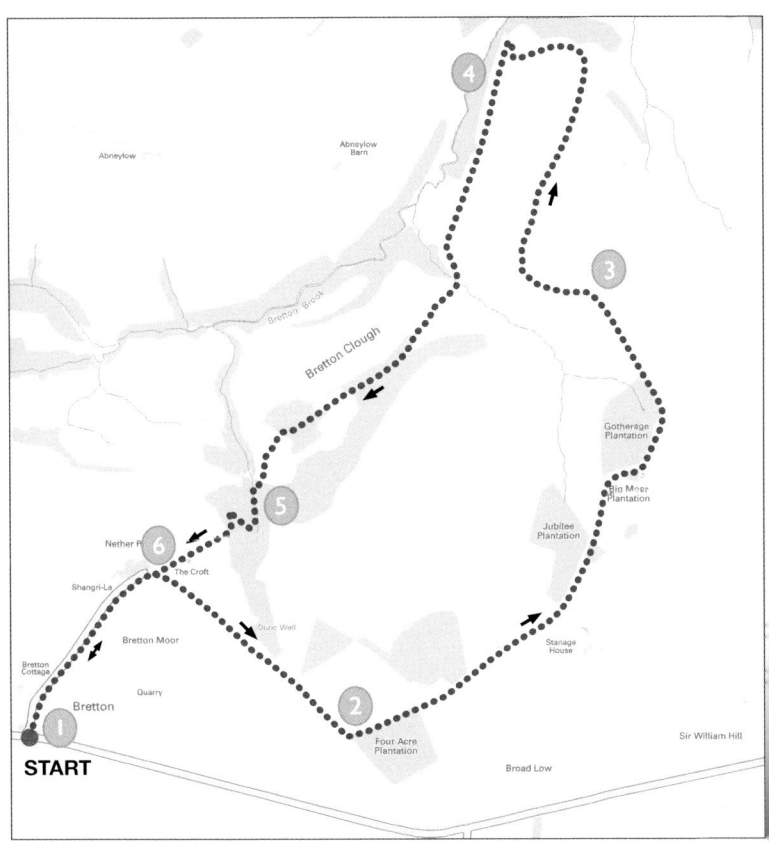

THE ROUTE

1. Facing the Barrel Inn, take the tarmac lane to the left of the building. Follow this down to a couple of cottages, enjoying the expansive views across to Abney Moor and Mam Tor. Stay on the lane, which becomes a rough track after The Croft, as far as a wooden ladder stile on the left of a gate, with a footpath sign to Stoke Ford.

2. Cross the stile and follow the track with a wood on your right. The track soon enters open ground. Follow it as far as the right-hand bend where the track heads up to farm buildings; do not continue along the track, instead keeping straight on along a grassy track, the original packhorse trail linking Eyam with Bradwell. Continue ahead, crossing two stiles alongside gates. Keeping a wall on the left with heather moorland on the right, descend to a stile on the left of a gate.

3. Cross this and continue descending the hillside, taking in the stunning views of Bretton Clough en route. The packhorse trail eventually degenerates into a narrow footpath as it descends more steeply into Bretton Clough through birch and oak woodland. At the end of the descent the path meets another that runs through Bretton Clough above a brook.

    Optional: To visit Stoke Ford turn right and follow the footpath down for 50 metres or so, then retrace your steps.

4. Turn left, or go straight on if returning from Stoke Ford. Follow the narrow footpath upstream above the brook through woodland dominated by silver birch, rowan and oak trees. The path passes through two gates, makes a short, steep climb, then passes through more open terrain before bending left into a narrow valley.

5. Cross a stile, pass through a gate and bear left to climb the steep slope by the zigzag path. Cross a stile by a gate at the top of the slope and keep following footpath, passing through another gate before arriving at the tarmac lane used at the start of the walk.

6. Turn right up the lane back to the inn.

8. DERWENT

THE ESSENTIALS

Distance: 6 miles (9.5 km)

Route: Medium; a fairly steep half-mile climb from the reservoir to the moor, and a shorter but steeper descent. Several gates, four stiles

Time: Approx. 4½ hours

Terrain: Tarmac for the first mile, then moorland paths and tracks .Short sections on the initial climb can be muddy after or during wet weather

Starting Point: Fairholmes Visitor Centre and car park in the Upper Derwent Valley. **Grid ref** SK 173 894, postcode S33 0AQ

Parking: Pay and display in the Visitor Centre car park

Food and Toilets: Refreshments at the Fairholmes Visitor Centre kiosk, the Ladybower Inn on the A57, and the Yorkshire Bridge Inn near the Ladybower Dam. Toilets at the Visitor Centre

Maps: OS Explorer 1 (Dark Peak);
OS Landranger 110 (Sheffield and Huddersfield)

INTRODUCTION

A walk among the stunning hill and valley scenery of the upper Derwent Valley, this route uses a combination of tracks and footpaths to pass over high ground overlooking the reservoirs. It also includes a walk alongside Derwent Reservoir and a descent by steps next to one of the dam's impressive stone towers.

Leaving the Visitor Centre at Fairholmes, the walk follows the lane that curves below the striking Derwent Dam, with its two turreted towers and a central section that becomes a massive cascade when the reservoir is full. The Derwent Dam was completed in 1916. Higher up the Derwent Valley is Howden Reservoir, whose dam has the same design and was completed in 1912. The work on the dams was done by a team of navvies who, along with their families, were housed in the temporary village of Birchinlee, known as Tin Town, the site of which is located on the west side of the Derwent Reservoir.

The two reservoirs with their dams were used during World War II for low-level flying practice for bombers preparing for the raid on the Ruhr Dams in Germany. The western tower of the Derwent Dam houses a small exhibition describing the epic raid. The feature film *The Dam Busters* also used the Derwent Valley and reservoirs for some of the flight sequences.

About a mile from the start of the walk, and just beyond the point that our route leaves Ladybower Reservoir and heads for the hills, is the site of the drowned village of Derwent. An information point adjacent to the site provides a picture of life as it was in the village.

Close by the high point on the walk is Pike Low, the site of a Bronze Age burial mound or barrow. Unfortunately there is no path up the 300 metres of heather moor leading to it, although those who can navigate with map and compass are free to walk to Pike Low since this is all open access country.

8. DERWENT WALK

THE ROUTE

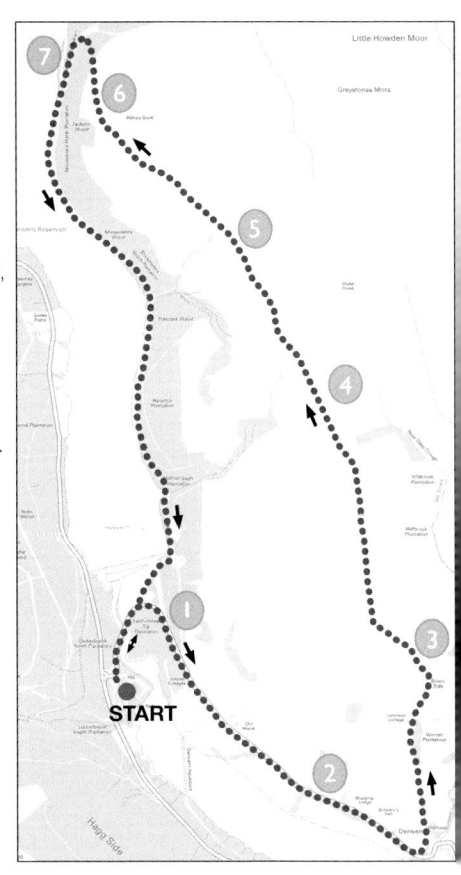

1. With your back to the kiosk, go left following the sign to Dams. Turn right on meeting the road, and follow as it curves below Derwent Dam and climbs to Jubilee Cottages. Continue above Ladybower Reservoir along the lane for a further ¾ mile to a footpath sign, gate and stile on the left immediately before the lane descends.

2. Cross the stile, follow the track towards Wellhead Barn, then bear left up the obvious path. Continue up via gates and a stile. After passing through the gate adjacent to a farm building keep ahead up the track signposted to Derwent Moors. The track bends left through a gate and continues up to another gate with a stile.

3. Cross the stile and follow the track up to the left. After 150 metres of ascent the track turns right and the going gets easier. (To the left, 300 metres up a heather slope but out of sight, is the ancient barrow on Pike Low.) Continue along the track and bear left as waymarked, eventually reaching a crossroads.

4. Keep straight on signposted to Abbey/Howden Dam. Where the track bends sharp right at a fence, keep ahead across a wooden stile. The footpath descends and arrives at a path crossroads with a sign embedded in a cairn.

5. Keep straight on for Howden Reservoir, taking the higher footpath at a fork just beyond the signpost. The path divides again in 200 metres; bear left down the slope to a wall. Bear right and follow the path beside the wall as it descends to a signpost.

6. Follow the path down to the right, signposted to Abney Grange. Pass through a gate and continue down through the wood to the track alongside Derwent Reservoir.

7. Turn left. Walk along the track for 1½ miles, then bear right through a gate by the dam. Turn right just beyond the dam wall to descend steps to the foot of the dam. Continue to the road, then bear right and retrace your steps to the Visitor Centre.

9. HAYFIELD

THE ESSENTIALS

Distance: 3¾ miles (6 km)

Route: Medium: prolonged climb over first mile. Several gates, no stiles

Time: Approx. 3½ hours

Terrain: Stony track near the start, then straightforward hill paths

Starting Point: Hayfield Countryside Centre car park, Hayfield. **Grid ref** SK 036 869, **postcode** SE22 2ES

Parking: Small charge for parking in Countryside Centre car park, as above

Food and Toilets: Rosie's Coffee and Tea Room on Kinder Road, and a choice of four pubs in Hayfield. Public toilets in the car park

Maps: OS Explorer 1 (Dark Peak);
OS Landranger 110 (Sheffield and Huddersfield)

INTRODUCTION

A steady climb along an old bridleway leads to a superb viewpoint overlooking Kinder Reservoir and the craggy basin forming the western flanks of Kinder Scout. A descent to the reservoir and a riverside footpath complete a fine excursion.

The village of Hayfield as it appears today is very much a product of the Industrial Revolution. In its heyday several cotton mills provided work for the villagers in spinning, weaving and calico printing. However, Hayfield's three-storied terraced houses testify to the existence of an earlier cottage industry based on woollen manufacture.

The village has four pubs, two of which, the Packhorse and the George Hotel, are said to date from the sixteenth century. The inns would have provided accommodation and sustenance to the 'jaggers' and their teams of twenty to thirty packhorses who assembled in the village before heading east across the high, desolate moors.

Hayfield has several other interesting buildings worth a second look. Fox Hall and the adjacent barn on Kinder Road date from 1625. Also on Kinder Road is the former home of Arthur Lowe, the actor most famed for his role as Captain Mainwaring in the TV show *Dad's Army*. A blue plaque hangs on the front of the cottage where he was born and brought up.

In the 1920s the railway link between Manchester and Hayfield brought five thousand people every weekend to enjoy the countryside around Kinder Scout. It was from Hayfield that a mass trespass on the grouse moors of Kinder Scout took place in 1932 to highlight the fact that walkers in England and Wales were denied access to areas of open country. Folk singer Ewan McColl celebrated the event in his song *The Manchester Rambler*.

9. HAYFIELD WALK

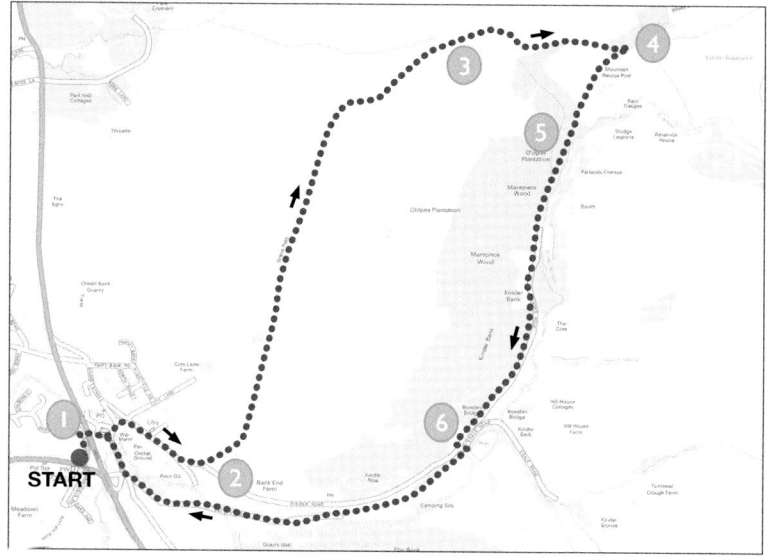

THE ROUTE

1. Facing the Countryside Centre, go right, cross the main road at the pedestrian crossing, and keep straight on beside the church to the road running through the village. Turn left, cross the bridge, then head up Bank Street. Bear right and continue up Kinder Road to the Snake Path bridleway on the left.

2. Turn left and follow the bridleway up, passing through several gates. Stay on the well-worn path, with fine views left across the valley to Lantern Pike. The angle of the slope gradually eases and the bridleway levels out and passes through a gate, where you enter National Trust land. The path bears right and climbs gradually towards a prominent white hut, the Shooting Cabin. Continue to a path crossroads.

3. Turn right to follow the footpath signposted to Snake Inn and Edale. In a short distance at a fingerpost follow the bridleway, the right fork. Stay on this as it descends the hillside, ignoring any other possibilities. Pass through a bridlegate and continue down to join the footpath that runs above the reservoir.

4. Turn right and follow the bridleway downhill. This becomes cobbled as it descends more steeply to merge with a tarmac road.

5. Either keep straight on along the road as far as Bowden Bridge car park, or, a more interesting option, turn left, follow the bridleway across the footbridge, then turn right immediately to walk with the River Kinder on your right. The footpath joins a minor road; follow this across the river and as far as Bowden Bridge car park.

6. Turn left opposite the car park, cross the bridge, then bear right along the campsite access road. Keep next to the river to follow the riverside path, then a road, back into the centre of Hayfield. Bear right down the main street and turn left immediately before the church to retrace your steps back to the car park.

10. GOYT VALLEY

THE ESSENTIALS

Distance: 2 miles (3.2 km). An easier walk of 1 mile (1.6 km) without the hill climb is included

Route: Medium; the first half mile is a steep hill climb. Easy if the alternative option is taken. Some gates, no stiles

Time: Approx. 2½ hours (approx. 1½ hours for the easier version)

Terrain: Footpaths throughout. A minor stream is crossed on stones which could be a problem in heavy rain

Starting Point: Errwood Hall car park in Goyt Valley, situated on the west side, and near the head of, Errwood Reservoir. **Grid ref** SJ 012 748, **postcode** SK17 6SX

Parking: Free parking in the Errwood Hall car park as above

Food and Toilets: The Cat and Fiddle Inn on the A537, or the Pavilion Gardens in Buxton. Public toilets 200 metres east of the Errwood Dam alongside Goyt Lane

Maps: OS Explorer 24 (White Peak);
OS Landranger 119 (Buxton and Matlock)

INTRODUCTION

This short but varied walk in the popular Goyt Valley starts with a short but steep climb to take in the striking moorland and reservoir scenery, then descends through delightful oak and pine woodland to explore the romantic ruins of Errwood Hall. An easier variation is included.

The Goyt is a deep river valley in the moorland west of Buxton. The word 'goyt' derives from the Old English 'gota', meaning a stream or river. Like the Upper Derwent Valley in the east of the Peak District, the upper valley of the River Goyt was dammed to form the two reservoirs of Fernilee and Errwood.

The Goyt Valley has been a popular tourist destination since Victorian times, when visitors came, much as they do nowadays, to enjoy and walk in this upland valley and on the moors that surround it. In Victorian times, however, the valley did not have its reservoirs and was home to a working community with farms, a paint works, a gunpowder factory, coal mines, a railway, a school, and the Victorian mansion of Errwood Hall.

The route of the walk climbs a moorland footpath for a view of the Goyt Valley, then descends Shooter's Clough to explore the ruins of Errwood Hall. This was a spectacular mansion built around 1840. It was the stately home of the Grimshawe family, who had a major influence on the valley in the nineteenth century, bringing prosperity to the small community.

A mile further up the valley is Goytsclough Quarry. It is reputed to be where the international haulage firm Pickford's started trading in the late seventeenth century. The means of haulage at that time was trains of packhorses in the charge of packhorsemen, or 'jaggers'. A browse at a map of the Peak District will reveal several references to jaggers, indicating routes that were used to crisscross the valleys, hills and moors of the Peak linking one market town to another.

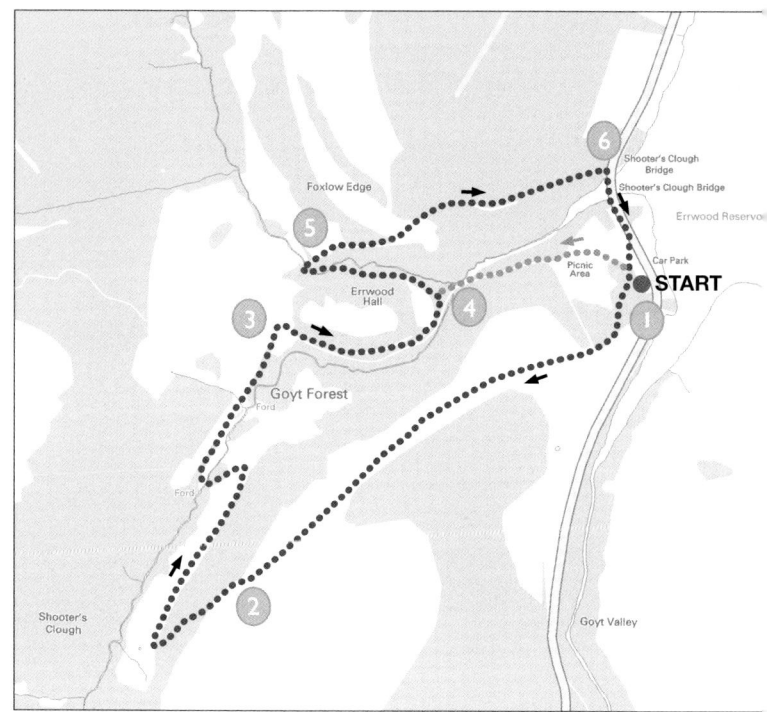

THE ROUTE

1. Facing the reservoir, walk to the right through the car park, and then turn right as signposted for Stake Side. The path climbs steeply. Continue through gate posts and keep straight on uphill for Stake Side. After half a mile of climbing the path reaches a signpost and gate.

2. Continue through the gate signed for Shooter's Clough. The path descends gradually through lovely oak woodland, doubling back to follow the stream's descent of the valley. Further down the path

doubles back to the left, signposted Erwood, crosses a minor stream via stones, then continues downhill with the stream now on your right. The path eventually joins a track.

3. Turn right for Errwood Car Park. In a short distance another track forks left through prominent gate posts.

4. Bear left here to follow the leafy track. This arrives at steps on the edge of the ruins of Errwood Hall.

5. After exploring the ruins, bear left along the woodland footpath with a stream down in a deep gully to the right. Continue along a wooden walkway that crosses the stream, and bear right up steps. Continue along Woodland Walk to where it joins another path.

6. Bear right along the continuation of Woodland Walk. This descends through pines and joins the road beside the reservoir. Turn right to finish.

Easier Walk

1. Head for the information board at the back of the car park. Continue along the footpath for Errwood Hall ruins. After crossing the stream, look for steps on the right. Climb the steps, turn right and soon the path bends to the left to the ruins of the hall. Continue with instructions 5. and 6. above.

MORE WALKING BOOKS FROM BRADWELL BOOKS FOR YOU TO ENJOY

FROM THIS SERIES

BRADWELL'S POCKET WALKING GUIDES
10 Walks up to 6 miles,
suitable for all the family

Somerset
Essex
The Yorkshire Dales

WALKS FOR ALL AGES
20 Walks up to 6 miles,
suitable for all the family

The Black Country
Cambridgeshire
Carmarthenshire
The Chilterns
Cheshire
Co Durham
Cornwall
On Dartmoor
Devon
Dorset
Essex
Exmoor
Greater Manchester
Hampshire
Herefordshire
Kent
The Lake District
Lancashire
Leicestershire and Rutland
Lincolnshire
London Greater
Norfolk
North East Wales
Northamptonshire
Northumberland
Nottinghamshire
The Peak District
The Scottish Borders
Snowdonia & North West Wales
Somerset
Staffordshire
East Sussex

West Sussex
Vale of Glamorgan & Bridgend South Wales
West Yorkshire
Wiltshire
The Yorkshire Dales

WALKS FOR ALL SEASONS
20 Walks up to 6 miles, suitable for all the family throughout the year

Lincolnshire
Nottinghamshire

BRADWELLS LONGER WALKS
20 More challenging walks of up to 12 miles suitable for the more experienced walker

On Dartmoor
The Peak District
The Yorkshire Dales

COMING OUT IN 2017

WALKS FOR ALL AGES
20 Walks up to 6 miles,
suitable for all the family

Pembrokeshire
Suffolk
South Downs National Park
North York Moors

BRADWELL WALKING GUIDES
8 Family walks
Buxton
The Monsal Trail

Available from your local bookshop or order online

bradwellbooks.co.uk